T0016381

Jugs & Punches

Easy-to-follow recipes

Steve Quirk

NEW HOLLAND

Introduction

From basic mixers through to exotic creations, there is nothing complicated about preparing and constructing jugs and punches, as you will soon discover.

Each recipe provides clear and uncomplicated directions, ensuring that even those with no experience will soon be mixing drinks with ease. Want to know how to chill a glass? How to layer ingredients? What bar equipment is required? All the answers you need are provided here, along with other useful tips for creating perfect punches and mixed drinks.

An approximate percentage of alcohol per volume (% alc/vol) content has been supplied for each alcoholic drink recipe, as well as how many standard drinks each contains.

These calculations are based on information believed to be accurate and reliable, although cannot be guaranteed due to the alcohol/volume variations between the different brands of spirits and liqueurs. These calculations should be used only as a guide.

The percentage of alcohol for all spirits and liqueurs required for drinks contained within this book are provided.

A note on Measures

1 dash	1ml
1 teaspoon	5g/5ml
1 tablespoon	15g/20ml
1 cup (liquid measures)	250ml (9fl oz)
Solid measures (vary, depending on substance)	
1 cup caster sugar	220g (8oz)

Total liquid amounts given for each recipe are approximates only.

How to construct your drinks

Layering

Layering a drink creates a great effect in the jug. Pour each ingredient over the back of a large spoon into your chosen jug, bowl or glass. This will allow the liquid to flow down the inside rim of the glass, creating a layering effect. Usually, the heavier ingredients are poured first.

Blending

When a blender is required, use only cracked or crushed ice in suitable blenders and blend until ingredients are evenly mixed.

Frosting

Frosting a glass adds a new dimension to whatever you are drinking. And it looks great too. You create a frosting by coating the rim of a glass with salt or sugar.

First, moisten the rim of a glass using a slice of lemon or orange. Next, hold the chosen glass by its base or stem upside down and rest gently on a flat plate containing salt or caster sugar and twist slightly.

If you press down too hard on the glass, you may end up with chunks of salt or sugar sticking to the rim.

Lemon is used for salt-frosted rims and orange for sugar-frosted rims unless otherwise stated.

Sugar syrup

To make sugar syrup, bring one cup of ordinary white sugar with one cup of water almost to the boil in a small saucepan, stirring continuously. Simmer until sugar is completely dissolved.

Remove from heat and allow to cool. Once cool, pour into a re-sealable container or a corked bottle and store in the refrigerator or behind your bar for regular use.

This syrup will now last indefinitely.

Sweet and sour mix

To make sweet and sour mix, bring one cup of sugar syrup to simmer then add half a cup of fresh lemon juice and half a cup of fresh lime juice.

Simmer until well mixed, stirring frequently, then remove from heat and allow to cool. Once cool, pour into a re-sealable container or corked bottle and store in the refrigerator for up to two weeks. Sweet and sour mix is also referred to as sour mix or bar mix.

How To chill a glass

Place bowls, jugs and glasses in a refrigerator to chill or place ice cubes into the glasses while drinks are being prepared. Discard these ice cubes before pouring unless otherwise instructed.

Fruit, peels and juices

Fruit slices and pieces will keep fresher and longer if covered with a damp, clean, linen cloth and refrigerated. Where citrus peel is required, cut the peel into required sizes and shave away the white membrane. Fruit and peels should be the last added ingredient to a cocktail or punch (garnish). When juices are required remember—fresh is best.

When using canned fruit and/or juices, transfer the can's contents into appropriate re-sealable containers and refrigerate.

Ice

It is important to maintain a well-stocked, clean ice supply, as most cocktails and punches require ice during construction.

To obtain crushed ice if you do not have access to an ice-crushing machine, place required ice onto a clean linen cloth and fold up. Place ice-filled cloth onto a hard surface and smash with a mallet—not a bottle.

Large blocks of ice are often required for punches. These ice blocks can be made easily by using two litre and/or four litre empty ice-cream containers.

Common Ingredients for
Jugs and Punches

SPIRITS

Bacardi

Bourbon

Brandy

Canadian Whisky

Cognac

Dark Rum

Gin

Irish Whiskey

Light Rum

Port

Rye Whiskey

Scotch Whisky

Sherry

Tequila

Vodka

LIQUEURS

Amaretto

Bailey's Irish Cream

Banana Liqueur

Bénédictine

Cherry Brandy

Cointreau

Crème De Cacao

Crème De Cassis

Crème De Menthe

Curaçao

Drambuie

Galliano

Grand Marnier

Kirsch

Malibu

Midori

Southern Comfort

Strawberry Liqueur

Tia Maria

Jugs and Punches

Punches are believed to have originated in Jamaica in the mid-seventeenth century and were rumbased.

The oldest-known punch contained only four ingredients: rum, orange juice, water and sugar.

Punches are great drinks for parties and place less demand on your time as you are not mixing individual drinks. They can be made, or at least prepared, before your guests arrive, giving you extra time to socialise and enjoy yourself. Punches can be made up simply in jugs or punch bowls, with fresh, seasonal fruit added and served with a ladle from a punch bowl or simply poured from a jug.

Ideally for cold punches, ingredients should be pre-chilled and large blocks of ice placed in the punch bowl will keep your punch cold. Empty ice-cream containers filled with water and frozen make ideal blocks of ice for punches. These large blocks will ensure that your punch will remain colder for a longer period of time for your guests to enjoy. Ice can be placed into jugs for the same effect. Effervescent

ingredients should be added last into a punch apart from the fruit, unless otherwise stated.

When preparing a jug or punch allow 150ml (5fl oz) of drink per guest. This should provide you with an adequate amount, as some guests may choose not to drink alcohol or indulge in your punch.

Tropical Punch

Makes 3.45l/116.65 | 10.8% alc/vol | 29.4 standard drinks

700ml (24fl oz) golden rum

500ml (17fl oz) apricot liqueur

750ml (26fl oz) grapefruit juice

750ml (26fl oz) pineapple juice

300ml (10fl oz) fresh orange juice

200ml (7fl oz) papaya juice

100ml (3⅓fl oz) mango juice

100ml (3⅓fl oz) passionfruit juice

50ml (1⅔fl oz) fresh lemon juice

Slices of orange

Slices of pineapple

1. **Pour rum, liqueur and juices into a punch bowl over ice.**
2. **Add slices of orange and pineapple.**
3. **Stir and serve.**

Fruit Punch

Makes 4.86l/164.33 | 6.5% alc/vol | 26.5 standard drinks

2L (64fl oz) white wine

250ml (8⅓fl oz) brandy

750ml (26fl oz) pineapple juice

500ml (17fl oz) fresh orange juice

240ml (8fl oz) fresh lemon juice

120ml (4fl oz) sugar syrup

1L (32fl oz) soda water

1½ cups peach slices

1 cup pineapple pieces

1 punnet cherries

1. **Pour brandy, orange juice, lemon juice and sugar into a chilled punch bowl. Add slices of peach, pieces of pineapple and cherries.**

2. **Stir and refrigerate for one hour.**

3. **Add ice, wine, pineapple juice and soda. Stir gently and serve.**

Mint Punch

Makes 1.97l/66.61fl oz | 3% alc/vol | 4.7 standard drinks

120ml (4fl oz) Gin

60ml (2fl oz) Green Crème De Menthe

1L (32fl oz) pineapple juice

500ml (17fl oz) grapefruit juice

240ml (8fl oz) fresh lemon juice

50ml (1⅔fl oz) sugar syrup

Fresh mint leaves

1. Pour gin, Crème De Menthe, juices and sugar syrup into a punch bowl over ice.
2. Stir well and float mint leaves on top, then serve.

Poor Man's Punch

Makes 5.15l/174.14 |4.5% alc/vol | 18.2 standard drinks

2L (64fl oz) red bordeaux wine

580ml (19fl oz) fresh lemon juice

285ml (9½ fl oz) raspberry syrup

285ml (9½ fl oz) sugar syrup

2L (64fl oz) soda water

1. Pour wine, juice, syrup and sugar syrup into a punch bowl over ice. Stir well and add soda.

2. Stir gently and serve.

West Indian Punch

Makes 6.08l/205.58fl oz | 15% alc/vol | 71.6 standard drinks

2L (64fl oz) light rum

750ml (26fl oz) banana liqueur

1L (32fl oz) fresh lemon juice

1L (32fl oz) fresh orange juice

1L (32fl oz) pineapple juice

150ml (5fl oz) sugar syrup

180ml (6fl oz) soda water

1 teaspoon cinnamon (ground)

1 teaspoon nutmeg (grated)

$\frac{1}{2}$ teaspoon cloves (ground)

Slices of banana

1. Pour sugar syrup and soda into a jug without ice. Add cinnamon, nutmeg and cloves.

2. Stir gently and pour into a punch bowl over a large block of ice.

3. Add remaining ingredients, stir and serve.

Punch Bowler

Makes 1.75l/59.17 | 16% alc/vol | 22.1 standard drinks

750ml (26fl oz) vodka

750ml (26fl oz) fresh orange juice

250ml (8⅓fl oz) grapefruit juice

Slices of orange

1. Pour vodka and juices into a punch bowl over ice then add slices of orange.

2. Stir and serve.

Orange Punch

Makes 3l/101.44fl oz | 9.3% alc/vol | 22 standard drinks

750ml (26fl oz) vodka

750ml (26fl oz) fresh orange juice

750ml (26fl oz) dry ginger ale

750ml (26fl oz) soda water

1. Pour vodka and juice into a punch bowl over ice then stir.

2. Add ginger ale and soda.

3. Stir gently and serve.

Rum and Fruit Juice Bowl

Makes 1.40l/47.33fl oz | 9.4% alc/vol | 10.5 standard drinks

360ml (12fl oz) dark rum

60ml (2fl oz) grenadine

300ml (10fl oz) fresh orange juice

300ml (10fl oz) pineapple juice

180ml (6fl oz) fresh lemon juice

180ml (6fl oz) coconut cream

30ml (1fl oz) sugar syrup

Maraschino cherries

Pieces of pineapple

1. **Pour rum, grenadine, juices, cream and sugar syrup into a punch bowl over ice.**

2. **Add cherries and pieces of pineapple.**

3. **Stir well and serve.**

Melon Ball Cup

Makes 1.36l/ 45.98fl oz | 12.5% alc/vol | 13.5 standard drinks

375ml (13fl oz) Midori

240ml (8fl oz) vodka

750ml (26fl oz) fresh orange juice or grapefruit juice

Slices of melon

Slices of orange

Strawberries

1. Pour Midori, vodka and juice into a jug over ice then add remaining ingredients.

2. Stir and serve.

Extra Kick Punch

Makes 3.31l/111.92fl oz | 8% alc/vol | 22.4 standard drinks

500ml (17fl oz) dark rum

250ml (8⅓fl oz) brandy

60ml (2fl oz) peach brandy

2L (64fl oz) spring water

250ml (8⅓fl oz) fresh lemon juice

250ml (8⅓fl oz) pineapple juice

1 cup brown sugar

1. **Pour water into a mixing bowl without ice. Add sugar then stir well to dissolve sugar.**
2. **Add remaining ingredients, stir and refrigerate to chill.**
3. **Pour into a punch bowl over a large block of ice and serve.**

Rum Punch

Makes 1.42l/48fl oz | 7.5% alc/vol | 9.1 standard drinks

300ml (10fl oz) Bacardi

180ml (6fl oz) fresh lemon juice

180ml (6fl oz) fresh orange juice

120ml (4fl oz) pineapple juice

750ml (26fl oz) dry ginger ale

Slices of orange

1. **Pour Bacardi and juices into a punch bowl over ice then stir.**

2. **Add ginger ale and stir gently.**

3. **Add slices of orange then serve.**

Citrus-Beer Punch

Makes 1.5l/50.72fl oz | 1.1% alc/vol | 1.5 standard drinks

750ml (26fl oz) light beer

500ml (17fl oz) sugar syrup

250ml (8⅓fl oz) grapefruit juice

8 fresh lemons (juiced and peeled)

Slices of lemon

1. Pour sugar syrup into a saucepan and bring to the boil then add lemon peel.

2. Remove from heat, cover and allow to stand for five minutes.

3. Strain into a jug and add juices then stir. Cover and refrigerate to chill.

4. Add beer and stir gently.

5. Pour into glass beer mugs over cracked ice and garnish with a slice of lemon for each serving.

Maui Wowie Punch

Makes 4.45l/150.47fl oz | 10.5% alc/vol | 37.3 standard drinks

1.7L (58fl oz) Malibu

500ml (17fl oz) Midori

1.125L (38fl oz) fresh lemon juice

1.125L (38fl oz) pineapple juice

Slices of orange

Slices of pineapple

1. Pour Malibu, Midori and juices into a punch bowl over ice then stir well.

2. Add slices of orange and pineapple then serve.

All American Punch

Makes 3.18l/107.52fl oz | 5.3% alc/vol | 13.3 standard drinks

450ml (15fl oz) Southern Comfort

450ml (15fl oz) fresh orange juice

90ml (3fl oz) fresh lime juice

30ml (1fl oz) maraschino cherry juice

1.8L (60fl oz) cola

360ml (12fl oz) soda water

Maraschino cherries

Slices of lime

Slices of orange

1. **Pour Southern Comfort and juices into a chilled punch bowl.**

2. **Stir well and add a large block of ice.**

3. **Add cola and soda then stir gently.**

4. **Add cherries, slices of lime and orange then serve.**

U-238 Punch

Makes 3.75l/126.80fl oz | 15% alc/vol | 44.4 standard drinks

750ml (26fl oz) light rum

750ml (26fl oz) vodka

750ml (26fl oz) fresh orange juice

750ml (26fl oz) pineapple juice

750ml (26fl oz) strawberry juice

2 cups pineapple pieces

2 cups strawberries

2 cups wedges of orange

1. Pour rum, vodka and juices into a punch bowl resting on a bed of ice then stir well.

2. Add pieces of pineapple, strawberries and wedges of orange then serve.

Pineapple and Orange Punch

Makes 1.86l/62.89fl oz | 7.5% alc/vol | 11 standard drinks

375ml (13fl oz) dry gin

375ml (13fl oz) fresh orange juice

180ml (6fl oz) fresh lemon juice

180ml (6fl oz) pineapple juice

750ml (26fl oz) lemonade or soda water

Slices of orange

Slices of pineapple

Strawberries

1. Pour gin and juices into a punch bowl over ice.
2. Add slices of orange, pineapple and strawberries.
3. Stir and add lemonade or soda as desired.
4. Stir gently and serve.

Peach on the Beach Punch

Makes 4.25l/143.70fl oz | 13.4% alc/vol | 44.9 standard drinks

1.75L (58fl oz) Malibu

1L (32fl oz) peach schnapps

1.5L (52fl oz) fresh orange juice

Slices of orange

Slices of peach

1. **Pour Malibu, schnapps and juice into a punch bowl over a large block of ice then stir.**

2. **Add slices of orange and peach then serve.**

Cannonball

Makes 3.98l/134.57fl oz | 9.5% alc/vol | 29.8 standard drinks

500ml (17fl oz) light rum

500ml (17fl oz) gin

1L (32fl oz) fresh orange juice

1L (32fl oz) pineapple juice

620ml (20fl oz) lemon-lime soda

360ml (12fl oz) strawberry soda

1. **Pour rum, gin and juices into a punch bowl resting on a bed of ice.**

2. **Stir well and add sodas.**

3. **Stir gently and serve.**

Malibu Party Punch

Makes 8.13l/274.90fl oz | 4.5% alc/vol | 28.8 standard drinks

1.75L (58fl oz) Malibu

2.25L (72fl oz) cranberry-raspberry juice

1.125L (38fl oz) fresh lime juice

3L (104fl oz) soda water

Slices of lime

Slices of orange

1. Pour Malibu and juices into a punch bowl over a large block of ice.

2. Add soda and stir gently.

3. Add slices of lime and orange then serve.

American Ice Tea

Makes 1.5l/50.72fl oz | 5% alc/vol | 5.9 standard drinks

300ml (10fl oz) triple sec

750ml (26fl oz) strong black tea (chilled)

450ml (15fl oz) fresh orange juice

1. **Pour triple sec and juice into a jug over ice then stir.**
2. **Add tea by layering on top and serve.**

Hall of Fame Punch

Makes 0.96l/32.46fl oz | 7% alc/vol | 5.3 standard drinks

180ml (6fl oz) vodka

60ml (2fl oz) grenadine

180ml (6fl oz) fresh orange juice

180ml (6fl oz) pineapple juice

180ml (6fl oz) sweet and sour mix

180ml (6fl oz) lemon-lime soda

Cherries

Slices of orange

1. **Pour Vodka, Grenadine, juices and sour mix into a jug over large amount of ice then stir well.**

2. **Add soda and stir gently.**

3. **Add cherries and slices of orange then serve.**

Dancing Dutchman

Makes 2.7l/91.29fl oz |3.9% alc/vol | 8.3 standard drinks

250ml (8⅓fl oz) white wine

125ml (4fl oz) vodka

75ml (2½fl oz) scotch whisky

1.25L (42fl oz) strawberry juice

750ml (26fl oz) peach nectar

250ml (8⅓fl oz) fresh lime juice

Cherries

1. **Pour juices and nectar into a blender over crushed ice. blend until slushy then add wine, vodka and whisky.**

2. **Blend and pour into a chilled punch bowl.**

3. **Add cherries and serve.**

Tropical Hooter Punch

Makes 3.61l/122.06fl oz | 12.3% alc/vol | 35 standard drinks

1.75L (58fl oz) Malibu

360ml (12fl oz) Midori

750ml (26fl oz) cranberry juice

750ml (26fl oz) pineapple juice

Cherries or cranberries

Slices of orange

Garnish with Minit

1. **Pour Malibu, Midori and juices into a punch bowl over ice then stir well.**

2. **Add cherries and slices of orange then serve.**

Vodka Bombay Punch

Makes 8.43l/285.05fl oz | 13.5% alc/vol | 89.7 standard drinks

4L (132fl oz) champagne

1L (32fl oz) vodka

1L (32fl oz) sherry

285ml (9$\frac{1}{2}$fl oz) curaçao

140ml (4$\frac{2}{3}$fl oz) maraschino liqueur

2L (64fl oz) soda water

Cherries

Slices of orange

1. Pour vodka, sherry, curaçao and liqueur into a punch bowl resting on a bed of ice.

2. Add cherries and slices of orange.

3. Stir then add soda and champagne.

4. Stir gently and serve.

Punch on the Nose

Makes 1.96l/66.27fl oz | 3.3% alc/vol | 7 standard drinks

750ml (26fl oz) white wine (chilled)

375ml (13fl oz) pineapple juice

90ml (3fl oz) fresh lemon juice

750ml (26fl oz) soda water

Dash orange syrup/cordial

1 paw paw (diced)

Slices of orange

Slices of pineapple

Strawberries

1. Pour juices and syrup into a blender over cracked ice then add diced paw paw.

2. Blend and pour into a chilled punch bowl.

3. Add wine and stir thoroughly then refrigerate for three hours.

4. Add ice, soda, slices of orange, pineapple and strawberries.

5. Stir gently and serve.

Mint Punch

Makes 1.97l/66.61fl oz | 3% alc/vol | 4.7 standard drinks

120ml (4fl oz) Gin

60ml (2fl oz) Green Crème De Menthe

1L (32fl oz) pineapple juice

500ml (17fl oz) grapefruit juice

240ml (8fl oz) fresh lemon juice

50ml (1⅔fl oz) sugar syrup

Fresh mint leaves

1. Pour gin, Crème De Menthe, juices and sugar syrup into a punch bowl over ice.
2. Stir well and float mint leaves on top, then serve.

Poor Man's Punch

Makes 5.15l/174.14 | 4.5% alc/vol | 18.2 standard drinks

2L (64fl oz) red bordeaux wine

580ml (19fl oz) fresh lemon juice

285ml (9½fl oz) raspberry syrup

285ml (9½fl oz) sugar syrup

2L (64fl oz) soda water

1. **Pour wine, juice, syrup and sugar syrup into a punch bowl over ice.**

2. **Stir well and add soda.**

3. **Stir gently and serve.**

Champagne Punch

Makes 1.10l/37.19fl oz | 11.5% alc/vol | 10 standard drinks

750ml (26fl oz) champagne

60ml (2fl oz) brandy

45ml ($1\frac{1}{2}$fl oz) cointreau

250ml ($8\frac{1}{3}$fl oz) fresh orange juice

Maraschino cherries

Pieces of pineapple

Slices of orange

1. Pour brandy, cointreau and juice into a punch bowl over ice. add cherries, pieces of pineapple and slices of orange.

2. Stir well and add champagne.

3. Stir gently and serve.

Bellini Punch

Makes 1.53l/51.73fl oz | 7.5% alc/vol | 14.4 standard drinks

1.5L (52fl oz) champagne

30ml (1fl oz) fresh lemon juice

10 fresh peaches (diced)

Slices of peach

1. **Pour juice into a blender over cracked ice and add diced peaches.**

2. **Blend and pour into a punch bowl over ice.**

3. **Add Champagne and stir gently.**

4. **Add slices of peach and serve.**

Party Punch

Makes 2.97l/100.42fl oz | 17% alc/vol | 39.8 standard drinks

1.5L (52fl oz) champagne

750ml (26fl oz) Southern Comfort

120ml (4fl oz) Jamaica rum

240ml (8fl oz) grapefruit juice

240ml (8fl oz) pineapple juice

120ml (4fl oz) fresh lemon juice

Slices of orange

1. Pour Southern Comfort, rum and juices into a punch bowl over ice then add slices of orange.
2. Stir well and add champagne.
3. Stir gently and serve.

Sunset Punch

Makes 3.1l/104.82fl oz | 11% alc/vol | 29.4 standard drinks

1.5L (52fl oz) champagne

240ml (8fl oz) Cointreau

180ml (6fl oz) maraschino liqueur

90ml (3fl oz) brandy

90ml (3fl oz) cherry brandy

500ml (17fl oz) fresh lemon juice

500ml (17fl oz) strong black tea (chilled)

1 cup caster sugar

24 maraschino cherries

2 fresh oranges (sliced)

1. **Pour juice into a chilled punch bowl and add sugar then stir well to dissolve.**

2. **Add Cointreau, liqueur, brandies and tea then stir.**

3. **Add a large block of ice and champagne then stir gently.**

4. **Add cherries and slices of orange then serve.**

Boston Punch

Makes 1.85l/62.55fl oz | 11.5% alc/vol | 16.8 standard drinks

750ml (26fl oz) champagne

280ml (9⅓fl oz) cider

140ml (4fl oz) brandy

90ml (3⅔fl oz) dark rum

60ml (2fl oz) Cointreau

120ml (4fl oz) fresh lemon juice

1 tablespoon sugar syrup

400ml (13⅓fl oz) soda water

1 apple (cut into wedges)

1. **Pour cider, brandy, rum, Cointreau, juice and sugar syrup into a punch bowl over ice then stir.**

2. **Add soda and champagne then stir gently.**

3. **Add wedges of apple and serve.**

Champagne Cup

Makes 0.85l/28.74fl oz | 13% alc/vol | 8.8 standard drinks

750ml (26fl oz) champagne

60ml (2fl oz) brandy

30ml (1fl oz) fresh lemon juice

15ml ($\frac{1}{2}$fl oz) sugar syrup

Pieces of pineapple

Slices of lemon

Slices of orange

Slices of strawberries

1. Pour juice and sugar syrup into a mixing glass without ice. stir well and pour into a jug over ice then add brandy.

2. Add pieces of pineapple, slices of lemon, strawberries and orange. stir and add champagne.

3. Stir gently and serve.

Vodka Bombay Punch

Makes 8.43l/285.05fl oz | 13.5% alc/vol | 89.7 standard drinks

4L (132fl oz) champagne

1L (32fl oz) vodka

1L (32fl oz) sherry

285ml (9$\frac{1}{2}$fl oz) curaçao

140ml (4$\frac{2}{3}$fl oz) maraschino liqueur

2L (64fl oz) soda water

Cherries

Slices of orange

1. Pour vodka, sherry, curaçao and liqueur into a punch bowl resting on a bed of ice.

2. Add cherries and slices of orange.

3. Stir then add soda and champagne.

4. Stir gently and serve.

Christmas Punch

Makes 4.86l/164.33fl oz | 18.2% alc/vol | 98.5 standard drinks

2L (64fl oz) champagne

750ml (26fl oz) brandy

750ml (26fl oz) rum

750ml (26fl oz) rye whiskey

375ml (13fl oz) Bénédictine

10ml ($\frac{1}{3}$fl oz) Angostura Bitters

1L (32fl oz) fresh orange juice

1L (32fl oz) strong black tea (chilled)

225ml (7$\frac{1}{2}$fl oz) sugar syrup

1 pineapple (diced)

1. **Pour brandy, rum, whiskey, Bénédictine, Bitters, juice, tea and sugar syrup into a mixing bowl without ice then add diced pineapple.**

2. **Stir well and pour into a punch bowl over a large block of ice then add champagne.**

3. **Stir gently and serve.**

Pimm's Punch

Makes 2.1l/71fl oz | 19% alc/vol | 33.5 standard drinks

750ml (26fl oz) champagne

375ml (13fl oz) Pimm's No.1

375ml (13fl oz) bourbon

180ml (6fl oz) light rum

180ml (6fl oz) sweet vermouth

300ml (10fl oz) fresh orange juice

75ml (2$\frac{1}{2}$fl oz) frozen orange concentrate

Slices of kiwi fruit

Slices of orange

Slices of pineapple

Strawberries

Garnish with Mint

1. Pour Pimm's, bourbon, rum and vermouth into a punch bowl over ice.

2. Add concentrate, slices of kiwi fruit, orange, pineapple and strawberries.

3. Stir well, then add juice and Champagne.

4. Stir gently and serve, garnish with mint.

Champagne Pineapple Punch

Makes 1.64l/55.45fl oz | 8.1% alc/vol | 11.9 standard drinks

750ml (26fl oz) champagne

500ml (17fl oz) sauterne

300ml (10fl oz) pineapple juice

90ml (3fl oz) fresh lemon juice

60g (2oz) caster sugar

200g (7oz) pineapple pieces

1. Pour sauterne and juices into a chilled jug.

2. Add sugar and pieces of pineapple. Stir well to dissolve sugar and refrigerate for two hours.

3. Pour into chilled wine glasses until three-quarters full, then top up with champagne.

4. Stir gently and serve.

Navy Punch

Makes 5.25l/177.52fl oz | 10.3% alc/vol | 67.3 standard drinks

4L (132fl oz) champagne

375ml (13fl oz) cognac

375ml (13fl oz) dark rum

375ml (13fl oz) peach brandy

120ml (4fl oz) fresh lemon juice

450g (15oz) caster sugar

4 pineapples (sliced)

Slices of lemon

Slices of orange

Slices of peach

1. **Place sugar and slices of pineapple into a chilled punch bowl then mix well.**

2. **Add cognac, rum, brandy and juice.**

3. **Stir well and refrigerate to chill. Add slices of lemon, orange and peach.**

4. **Add champagne, stir gently and serve.**

Kissing the Bride Punch

Makes 1.68l/56.80fl oz | 14.8% alc/vol | 19.8 standard drinks

1.5L (52fl oz) champagne

180ml (6fl oz) cognac

1 tablespoon icing sugar

1 punnet strawberries

1. Place strawberries into a chilled punch bowl and sprinkle sugar over strawberries.

2. Add cognac and refrigerate for eight hours.

3. Add champagne, stir gently and serve.

Champagne Rum Punch

Makes 4.75l/160.61fl oz | 20% alc/vol | 75 standard drinks

1L (32fl oz) añejo rum

1L (32fl oz) light rum

750ml (26fl oz) champagne

750ml (26fl oz) sweet vermouth

1L (32fl oz) fresh orange juice

250ml (8⅓fl oz) cranberry juice

2 fresh oranges (sliced thinly)

1. **Pour Rums, vermouth and juices into a chilled punch bowl.**
2. **Stir well and add a large block of ice.**

Gin Punch

Makes 1.59l/53.76fl oz | 23.5% alc/vol | 29.5 standard drinks

750ml (26fl oz) gin

125ml (4fl oz) brandy

125ml (4fl oz) Cointreau

90ml (3fl oz) fresh lemon juice

500ml (17fl oz) lemonade

Cucumber strips

Slices of lemon

Slices of orange

1. Pour gin, brandy, Cointreau and juice into a punch bowl over ice, then stir.
2. Add remaining ingredients, stir gently and serve.

Vodka Knockout Punch

Makes 2.4l/81.15fl oz | 19% alc/vol | 36.1 standard drinks

750ml (26fl oz) vodka

500ml (17fl oz) champagne

375ml (13fl oz) Midori

180ml (6fl oz) banana liqueur

600ml (20fl oz) fresh cream (chilled)

Slices of banana

Slices of melon

Strawberries

1. Pour vodka, Midori, liqueur and cream into a punch bowl over ice.
2. Stir well then add slices of banana, melon and strawberries.
3. Add champagne, stir gently and serve.

Ginger Punch

Makes 1.97l/66.61fl oz | 6.5% alc/vol | 10.1 standard drinks

700ml (24fl oz) dry white wine

120ml (4fl oz) golden rum

300ml (10fl oz) fresh orange juice

150ml (5fl oz) grapefruit juice

700ml (24fl oz) dry ginger ale

1. Pour wine, rum and juices into a jug without ice.

2. Stir well and refrigerate for two hours.

3. Add ginger ale, stir gently and serve.

Tequila Punch

Makes 4.75l/160.61fl oz | 17.5% alc/vol | 65.6 standard drinks

3L (104fl oz) sauterne (chilled)

1L (32fl oz) tequila (chilled)

750ml (26fl oz) champagne

2kg (4$\frac{1}{2}$lb) fresh fruit (diced)

1. Pour sauterne and tequila into a punch bowl over ice then add diced fruit.

2. Stir well and add champagne.

3. Stir gently and serve.

Red Wine Jug

Makes 3.28l/110.90fl oz | 12% alc/vol | 31.1 standard drinks

1.5L (52fl oz) red wine

750ml (26fl oz) port

375ml (13fl oz) cherry brandy

450ml (15fl oz) fresh orange juice

120ml (4fl oz) sugar syrup

90ml (3fl oz) fresh lemon juice

Maraschino cherries

Slices of lemon

Slices of orange

1. **Pour wine, port, brandy, juices and sugar syrup into a jug over ice then add remaining ingredients.**

2. **Stir and add soda water to taste, if desired.**

3. **Stir gently then serve.**

Fourth of July Punch

Makes 4.84l/163.65fl oz | 11.4% alc/vol | 50.3 standard drinks

2.25L (72fl oz) red wine (chilled)

750ml (26fl oz) brandy

750ml (26fl oz) champagne

720ml (24fl oz) fresh lemon juice

375ml (13fl oz) strong black tea (chilled)

1kg (2lb 4oz) caster sugar

Slices of lemon

1. Pour juice into a chilled punch bowl and add sugar.
2. Stir well to dissolve sugar and fill bowl with ice. Add wine, brandy and tea.
3. Stir and add champagne then stir gently.
4. Serve in chilled goblets with a slice of lemon as garnish for each serving.

Rose Jug

Makes 4.23l/143.03fl oz | 8.5% alc/vol | 28.4 standard drinks

3L (104fl oz) rosé wine (chilled)

540ml (18fl oz) cranberry liqueur

120ml (4fl oz) california brandy

570ml (19fl oz) soda water

16 thin pineapple slices

16 thin lemon slices

1 punnet strawberries

1. **Pour wine, liqueur and brandy into a jug and put in large blocks of ice.**

2. **Add pineapple slices, lemon slices and strawberries.**

3. **Stir and refrigerate for one hour.**

4. **Add soda, stir gently and serve.**

Pineapple Punch

Makes 2.72l/91.97fl oz | 7.5% alc/vol | 16.1 standard drinks

1.5L (52fl oz) oselle

30ml (1fl oz) gin

30ml (1fl oz) maraschino liqueur

5ml (⅙fl oz) Angostura Bitters

30ml (1fl oz) grenadine

90ml (3fl oz) fresh lemon juice

30ml (1fl oz) pine syrup/cordial

1L (32fl oz) soda water

½ fresh lemon (sliced)

Slices of pineapple

1. **Pour moselle, gin, liqueur, Bitters, grenadine, juice and syrup into a punch bowl resting on a bed of ice then stir well.**

2. **Add soda and stir gently.**

3. **Add slices of lemon and pineapple.**

4. **Stir gently and serve.**

Cold Duck

Makes 4.5l/151.16fl oz | 12% alc/vol | 42.6 standard drinks

3L (104fl oz) white wine

1.5L (52fl oz) champagne

Peel of 2 lemons

1. Place lemon peels into a punch bowl resting on a bed of ice and add wine.

2. Add champagne and stir gently.

3. Allow to stand for five minutes then remove peels from punch and serve.

Brandy Punch

Makes 3.12l/105.49fl oz | 20% alc/vol | 49.2 standard drinks

1.5L (52fl oz) brandy

250ml (8⅓fl oz) curaçao

60ml (2fl oz) grenadine

500ml (17fl oz) sugar syrup

450ml (15fl oz) fresh lemon juice

360ml (12fl oz) fresh orange juice

Slices of lemon

Slices of orange

1. Pour brandy, curaçao, grenadine, sugar syrup and juices into a punch bowl over ice.

2. Add slices of lemon and orange.

3. Stir well and serve.

Sun Burn Punch

Makes 4.5l/152.16fl oz | 12.3% alc/vol | 43.7 standard drinks

1.5L (52fl oz) vodka

1.5L (52fl oz) cranberry juice

1.5L (52fl oz) grapefruit juice

Cherries

Slices of lime

1. Pour vodka and juices into a punch bowl over a large block of ice then stir well.
2. Add cherries and slices of lime then serve.

Brandy Egg Nog Bowl

Makes 4.11l/138.97fl oz | 7.3% alc/vol | 27.3 standard drinks

750ml (26fl oz) cognac

120ml (4fl oz) Jamaica rum

3L (104fl oz) fresh milk (chilled)

240ml (8fl oz) thick cream (chilled)

125g (4¹⁄₂oz) sugar

12 fresh eggs

Nutmeg

1. Separate eggs; pour egg yolks into a mixing bowl and add sugar.

2. Beat well and pour into a chilled punch bowl. Add cognac, rum, milk and cream.

3. Beat well and refrigerate for two hours.

4. Pour egg whites into a clean mixing bowl and beat until stiff just prior to serving.

5. Fold whites into punch until thoroughly blended and sprinkle nutmeg on top then serve.

Tropical Punch No. 2

Makes 8l/270.51fl oz | 14.5% alc/vol | 95.8 standard drinks

4.5L (150fl oz) white wine

1L (32fl oz) light rum

500ml (17fl oz) banana liqueur

500ml (17fl oz) dark rum

1L (32fl oz) fresh orange juice

500ml (17fl oz) fresh lemon juice

450g (1lb) brown sugar

5 bananas (sliced)

1 pineapple (diced)

Fresh fruit (diced)

1. **Pour wine and juices into a chilled punch bowl. add sugar, slices of banana and diced pineapple.**

2. **Cover and allow to stand for 12 hours. strain into a chilled punch bowl then add rums and liqueur.**

3. **Add a large block of ice and refrigerate for one hour. add diced fruit, stir gently and serve.**

Charleston Punch

Makes 7.25l/245.15fl oz | 12.5% alc/vol | 74.5 standard drinks

3L (104fl oz) champagne

750ml (26fl oz) brandy

500ml (17fl oz) dark rum

300ml (10fl oz) peach brandy

1.5L (52fl oz) soda water

1L (32fl oz) green tea (chilled)

3 cups sugar

10 fresh limes (sliced thinly)

1 pineapple (sliced thinly)

1. Pour brandy into a punch bowl then add slices of lime and pineapple.

2. Cover and allow to marinate overnight. add rum, peach brandy, tea and sugar.

3. Stir well to dissolve sugar and refrigerate for three hours.

4. Add soda and champagne. stir gently and serve.

Sangria

Makes 1.29l/43.62fl oz | 10.5% alc/vol | 10.7 standard drinks

750ml (26fl oz) red wine

120ml (4fl oz) brandy

50ml (1⅔fl oz) sugar syrup

375ml (13fl oz) soda water

Slices of lemon

Slices of lime

Slices of orange

1. Pour wine, brandy and sugar into a jug over ice.

2. Add slices of lemon, lime and orange then stir.

3. Add soda, stir gently and serve.

Sangria Especiale

Makes 2.65l/89.60fl oz | 13.2% alc/vol | 28.7 standard drinks

1.5L (52fl oz) red wine

750ml (26fl oz) champagne

120ml (4fl oz) cognac

120ml (4fl oz) gin

90ml (3fl oz) fresh orange juice

75ml (2$\frac{1}{2}$fl oz) fresh lemon juice

$\frac{1}{2}$ cup caster sugar

Slices of lemon

Slices of orange

1. Pour wine, cognac, gin and juices into a punch bowl over ice then add sugar.

2. Stir well and add champagne then stir gently.

3. Add slices of lemon and orange then serve.

White Sangria

Makes 1.29l/43.62fl oz | 10.5% alc/vol | 10.7 standard drinks

750ml (26fl oz) white wine

120ml (4fl oz) brandy

50ml (1⅔fl oz) sugar syrup

375ml (13fl oz) soda water

Slices of lemon

Slices of lime

Slices of orange

1. **Pour wine, brandy and sugar into a jug over ice.**

2. **Add slices of lemon, lime and orange then stir.**

3. **Add soda, stir gently and serve.**

Boston Punch

Makes 1.85l/62.55fl oz | 11.5% alc/vol | 16.8 standard drinks

750ml (26fl oz) champagne

280ml (9⅓fl oz) cider

140ml (4fl oz) brandy

90ml (3⅔fl oz) dark rum

60ml (2fl oz) Cointreau

120ml (4fl oz) fresh lemon juice

1 tablespoon sugar syrup

400ml (13⅓fl oz) soda water

1 apple (cut into wedges)

1. Pour cider, brandy, rum, Cointreau, juice and sugar syrup into a punch bowl over ice then stir.

2. Add soda and champagne then stir gently.

3. Add wedges of apple and serve.

Buddha Punch

Makes 2.29l/77.43fl oz | 7.5% alc/vol | 13.6 standard drinks

750ml (26fl oz) champagne

250ml (8⅓fl oz) Rhine riesling

90ml (3fl oz) curaçao

90ml (3fl oz) rum

Dash Angostura Bitters

180ml (6fl oz) fresh lemon juice

180ml (6fl oz) fresh orange juice

750ml (26fl oz) soda water

Fresh mint leaves

Twists of lemon peel

1. **Pour riesling, curaçao, rum, Bitters and juices into a punch bowl over a large block of ice.**

2. **Stir and add soda. Add mint leaves, lemon peel and champagne.**

3. **Stir gently and serve.**

Mint Julep Punch

Makes 5.19l/175.49fl oz | 6% alc/vol | 25.8 standard drinks

820ml (28fl oz) bourbon

1.5L (52fl oz) pineapple juice

1L (32fl oz) spring water

120ml (4fl oz) fresh lime juice

1.75L (58fl oz) lemon-lime soda

1 cup set mint jelly (made from jelly crystals)

Slices of lime

Sprigs of fresh mint

1. Pour 500ml (17fl oz) water into a saucepan and add jelly.

2. Heat slowly stirring continuously to melt jelly then remove from heat and allow to cool.

3. Add bourbon, juices and remaining 500ml (17fl oz) water.

4. Stir and refrigerate to chill.

5. Pour into a punch bowl over a large block of ice and add soda then stir gently.

6. Add slices of lime and sprigs of mint then serve.

Somerset Punch

Makes 1.87l/63.23fl oz | 5% alc/vol | 7.4 standard drinks

1L (32fl oz) dry cider

150ml (5fl oz) dry white wine

60ml (2fl oz) apple brandy

150ml (5fl oz) apple juice

150ml (5fl oz) fresh orange juice

60ml (2fl oz) fresh lemon juice

300ml (10fl oz) dry ginger ale

Strawberries (sliced)

1. Pour cider, wine, brandy and juices into a punch bowl over a large block of ice.

2. Stir and add ginger ale.

3. Add sliced strawberries, stir gently and serve.

Texas Bar Punch

Makes 3.5l/ 118.34 | 7.7% alc/vol | 21.3 standard drinks

1.5L (52fl oz) ruby port

1L (32fl oz) dry ginger ale

1L (32fl oz) lemon-lime soda

1 fresh lemon (sliced)

1 fresh orange (sliced)

1. Pour port, ginger ale and soda into a chilled punch bowl.

2. Stir gently and add a large block of ice.

3. Add slices of lemon and orange then serve.

Cider Fizz

Makes 1.58l/53.42fl oz | 4.1% alc/vol | 6.3 standard drinks

1L (32fl oz) cider

90ml (3fl oz) rum

360ml (12fl oz) fresh orange juice

120ml (4fl oz) fresh lemon juice

15ml ($\frac{1}{2}$fl oz) spring water

350g (12oz) caster sugar

2 tablespoons icing sugar

White of 3 eggs

Pinch of salt

1. Pour cider into a saucepan and add caster sugar then gently heat to a simmer whilst stirring frequently.

2. Remove from heat and refrigerate to cool.

3. Pour into a chilled jug then add rum and juices.

4. Stir and refrigerate for one hour.

5. Pour water and egg whites into a mixing bowl then add salt.

6. Beat well and add icing sugar then beat again.

7. Pour cider mixture into bowl over egg white mixture and beat.

8. Pour combined mixtures into a clean chilled jug and serve.

Midori Punch

Makes 2.25l/76.08fl oz | 19.5% alc/vol | 34.6 standard drinks

750ml (26fl oz) Midori

750ml (26fl oz) vodka

750ml (26fl oz) lemonade

Slices of lemon

Slices of orange

1. Pour Midori and Vodka into a punch bowl over ice.

2. Add slices of lemon and orange.

3. Stir and add lemonade.

4. Stir gently and serve.

Chocolate Punch

Makes 1.37l/46.32fl oz | 4.5% alc/vol | 4.9 standard drinks

375ml (13fl oz) Bailey's Irish Cream

1L (32fl oz) fresh milk (chilled)

Nutmeg

1. **Pour Bailey's and milk into a blender over crushed ice.**

2. **Blend until smooth and pour into a chilled jug then serve with nutmeg lightly sprinkled over each serving.**

Chocolate Cocktail Punch

Makes 0.24l/8.11fl oz | 19% alc/vol | 4.5 standard drinks

180ml (6fl oz) port

60ml (2fl oz) Yellow Chartreuse

Yolk of 4 eggs

4 teaspoons dark chocolate (grated)

Slices of kiwi fruit

1. **Pour port, Chartreuse and egg yolks into a blender over cracked ice then add grated chocolate.**

2. **Blend and strain into a jug.**

3. **Pour into chilled cocktail glasses and garnish with a slice of kiwi fruit with each serving.**

Run and Go Naked

Makes 6l/202.88fl oz | 8.4% alc/vol | 39.8 standard drinks

4.5L (150fl oz) beer

750ml (26fl oz) vodka (chilled)

750ml (26fl oz) lemonade concentrate

1. Pour beer into a chilled punch bowl and add vodka.

2. Add concentrate, stir gently and serve

Malibu Tequila Punch

Makes 4.25l/143.70fl oz | 17.6% alc/vol | 59 standard drinks

1.75L (58fl oz) Malibu

1L (32fl oz) tequila

1.5L (52fl oz) pineapple juice

Slices of pineapple

1. Pour Malibu, Tequila and juice into a punch bowl over a large block of ice then stir well.

2. Add slices of pineapple and serve.

Malibu Mimosa Punch

Makes 4.25l/143.70fl 0z | 11.5% alc/vol | 38.6 standard drinks

1.75L (58fl oz) Malibu

1L (32fl oz) champagne

1.5L (52fl oz) fresh orange juice

Slices of orange

1. Pour Malibu and juice into a punch bowl over a large block of ice then stir.

2. Add champagne and stir gently.

3. Add slices of orange and serve

Hot Whiskey Punch

Makes 1.75l/59.17fl oz | 20% alc/vol | 31.6 standard drinks

1L (32fl oz) blended or Irish whiskey

750ml (26fl oz) spring water

1 cup sugar

1 fresh lemon (peeled and sliced)

8 whole cloves

2 cinnamon sticks

1. Pour water into a saucepan then add sugar, lemon peel, cloves and cinnamon sticks.

2. Bring to the boil, stirring frequently and simmer for 10 minutes.

3. Remove from heat and strain into a clean saucepan.

4. Add whiskey and heat to a simmer without boiling then remove from heat.

5. Pour into coffee glasses over a silver spoon (to prevent glasses cracking) and add a slice of lemon to each serving.

Winter Wine

Makes 0.47l/15.89fl oz | 13% alc/vol | 5 standard drinks

350ml (11⅔fl oz) red wine

60ml (2fl oz) cognac

60ml (2fl oz) spring water

1 tablespoon honey

Pinch of cinnamon

Slices of lemon

1. Pour wine, cognac, water and honey into a saucepan then add cinnamon.

2. Heat to a simmer without boiling, stirring frequently, then remove from heat and pour into wine glasses over a silver spoon (to prevent glasses cracking).

3. Garnish with a slice of lemon for each serving.

Mulled Port Punch

Makes 1.25l/42.26fl oz | 10.5% alc/vol | 10.9 standard drinks

750ml (26fl oz) tawny port

500ml (17fl oz) spring water

$\frac{1}{4}$ cup sugar

2 fresh oranges (peeled and sliced)

12 whole cloves

cinnamon stick

$\frac{1}{2}$ teaspoon allspice (ground)

$\frac{1}{2}$ teaspoon mace (ground)

$\frac{1}{2}$ teaspoon nutmeg (grated)

1. Pour water into a saucepan then add sugar, orange peel, cloves, a cinnamon stick, allspice, mace and nutmeg.

2. Bring to the boil stirring frequently to dissolve sugar then simmer for 10 minutes, stirring occasionally.

3. Remove from heat and strain into a small saucepan.

4. Add port and heat to a simmer without boiling whilst stirring occasionally then remove from heat.

5. Pour into coffee glasses over a silver spoon (to prevent glasses cracking) and add a slice of orange to each serving.

Brown Betty

Makes 2.41l/81.49fl oz | 9% alc/vol | 18 standard drinks

1.5L (52fl oz) amber ale

375ml (13fl oz) brandy

540ml (18fl oz) spring water

½ cup brown sugar

1 fresh lemon (sliced)

4 whole cloves

Cinnamon stick

½ teaspoon ginger (ground)

½ teaspoon nutmeg (grated)

1. Pour water into a saucepan then add sugar, cloves, a cinnamon stick, ginger and nutmeg.

2. Bring to the boil, stirring frequently to dissolve sugar.

3. Simmer for 10 minutes, stirring occasionally, then add ale and brandy.

4. Heat to a simmer without boiling, stirring frequently, then remove from heat and pour into pre-warmed beer mugs over a silver spoon (to prevent mugs cracking).

5. Add a slice of lemon to each serving.

Coffee-Port Punch

Makes 0.75l/25.36fl oz | 18.3% alc/vol | 10.8 standard drinks

250ml (8⅓fl oz) dark rum

250ml (8⅓fl oz) white port

250ml (8⅓fl oz) hot black coffee

Sugar to taste

1. Pour rum, port and coffee into a saucepan.

2. Heat to drinking temperature without boiling whilst stirring occasionally then add sugar to taste and stir to dissolve sugar.

3. Remove from heat and pour into coffee glasses over a silver spoon (to prevent glasses cracking) then serve.

Glögg

Makes 2l/67.62fl oz | 18% alc/vol | 28.4 standard drinks

750ml (26fl oz) red wine

750ml (26fl oz) medium sherry

375ml (13fl oz) brandy

8ml ($^1\!/_4$fl oz) Angostura Bitters

120ml (4fl oz) sugar syrup

Almonds

Raisins

1. Pour wine, sherry, brandy, Bitters and sugar syrup into a saucepan then heat to a simmer without boiling whilst stirring frequently.

2. Remove from heat and pour into pre-warmed beer mugs that contain an almond and raisin; pour over a silver spoon (to prevent mugs cracking) then serve

Carry Nation Punch

Makes 3.95l/133.56fl oz

1.75L (58fl oz) dry ginger ale

1L (32fl oz) fresh orange juice

720ml (24fl oz) fresh lemon juice

240ml (8fl oz) pineapple juice

240ml (8fl oz) sugar syrup

Slices of lemon

Slices of orange

1. **Pour juices and sugar syrup into a chilled punch bowl then stir.**

2. **Add a large block of ice and ginger ale then stir gently.**

3. **Add slices of lemon and orange then serve.**

Granny's Punch

Makes 3l/101.44fl oz

750ml (26fl oz) cranberry juice

750ml (26fl oz) pineapple juice

750ml (26fl oz) lemonade

750ml (26fl oz) lemon-lime soda

1. Pour juices into a punch bowl over a large block of ice and stir.

2. Add lemonade and soda.

3. Stir gently and serve.

Seven-Up Punch

Makes 3.56l/120.37fl oz

2L (64fl oz) 7-Up

750ml (26fl oz) fresh orange juice

500ml (17fl oz) spring water

250ml (8⅓fl oz) pineapple juice

60ml (2fl oz) fresh lemon juice

½ cup caster sugar

4 cinnamon sticks

1. Pour water into a saucepan then add sugar and cinnamon sticks.

2. Heat to a simmer with out boiling, stirring occasionally, and allow to simmer for five minutes.

3. Remove from heat and allow to cool to room temperature then refrigerate to chill.

4. Pour into a punch bowl resting on a bed of ice and add juices then stir well.

5. Add 7-Up, stir gently and serve.

Big Party Punch

Makes 6.45l/218.10fl oz

2.8L (96fl oz) pineapple juice

1.75L (58fl oz) dry ginger ale

820ml (28fl oz) soda water

720ml (24fl oz) fresh orange juice

360ml (12fl oz) fresh lemon juice

2 cups sugar

2 cups strawberries

½ cup fresh mint leaves

Slices of lemon

Slices of orange

1. **Pour juices into a blender without ice and add sugar. Blend well and add mint leaves.**

2. **Pour into a chilled punch bowl and refrigerate for two hours.**

3. **Add a large block of ice and ginger ale.**

4. **Add soda and stir gently.**

5. **Add strawberries, slices of lemon and orange then serve.**

Carry Nation Punch

Makes 3.95l/133.56fl oz

1.75L (58fl oz) dry ginger ale

1L (32fl oz) fresh orange juice

720ml (24fl oz) fresh lemon juice

240ml (8fl oz) pineapple juice

240ml (8fl oz) sugar syrup

Slices of lemon

Slices of orange

1. Pour juices and sugar syrup into a chilled punch bowl then stir.

2. Add a large block of ice and ginger ale then stir gently.

3. Add slices of lemon and orange then serve.

Angel Punch

Makes 5.48l/185.30fl oz

2L (64fl oz) white grape juice

1.75L (58fl oz) soda water

1L (34fl oz) strong green tea (chilled)

480ml (16fl oz) fresh lemon juice

250ml (8⅓fl oz) sugar syrup

1. Pour juices, tea and sugar into a chilled punch bowl.

2. Stir well and refrigerate to chill.

3. Add a large block of ice and soda.

4. Stir gently and serve.

Index

NewHollandPublishers

 @newhollandpublishers